C000186473

Toddler tips
for mums and dads

Daisy Hay

TODDLER TIPS FOR MUMS AND DADS

Illustrations by Alex Hallatt

Summersdale Publishers Ltd
46 West Street
Chichester
West Sussex
PO19 1RP
UK

www.summersdale.com

Printed and bound by Tien Wah Press, Singapore

ISBN: 1-84024-647-2
ISBN 13: 978-1-84024-647-6

Contents

Introduction

Congratulations! You're now the proud parent of a toddler. You've done the sleepless nights, the endless feeding, the non-stop nappy changing and you're still alive... just. But before you get comfy in front of the sofa with a bottle of wine you might want to read this book, because if you thought that was bad, things are about to get a whole lot worse.

You won't remember much of your own life as a toddler – most likely because you spent far too much time getting stuck in things, screaming and falling over and have purposefully banished these 'glory' days from your memory. Probably for the best, otherwise you'd be off that sofa in a shot and out the front door.

But don't panic. It isn't all bad. The toddler years are full of fun firsts. First word, first step, first visit to A&E... and the first time you realise that breaking down the bathroom door that your child's locked shut isn't as easy as the Hulk makes it look.

Be afraid... be VERY afraid...

Crawl Before You Can Walk

You know your baby's a toddler when:

You're on first name terms with all the nurses at the local casualty department.

You know your baby's a toddler when:

Your living room resembles
a Toys R Us January sale.

Giveaways that you're a toddler's parent

Mums:

You can often be seen stalking supermarket aisles – frantically searching for your adventurous child.

You can finally fit back
into your skinny jeans
because you spend
all day worrying and
running and never
have time to eat.

Dads:

You have started carrying a condom at all times because the thought of being put through this again is just too frightening.

Your shoulders have
become the new base
camp for a small mass
of unwashed, sulky,
overgrown baby that
doesn't want to go to bed.

Good advice from other parents

'Don't lose your temper, it means they're winning.'

'You shouldn't leave your child in the ball pool all afternoon, even if you really did need a few hours "me" time.'

'This kitchen is a deathtrap! You should cover that sharp edge with a pillow and some masking tape.'

Toddler Take-over preparation checklist: the toddler's coming, so make sure you're ready!

Rip up your new carpets and put your old ones back down. All those exotic new stains will look right at home.

Hide all toxic chemicals, medication and dangerous objects in places even you'll forget to look when the tantrums become too much.

Watch as many of your favourite TV dramas as possible – from now on, every programme you watch will have a sing-along segment and annoying adults dressed in costumes.

Things you will now say all the time

'You're sitting two feet away from the potty, and you're telling me you couldn't make it?!'

'Take that out of
your mouth!'

[Whilst feeding your toddler baby mush]

'This actually looks quite nice.'

'Step away from the boiling water!'

Top Toddler Management Tips

Rules of thumb-sucking

Be warned: dummies are quietening devices sent from the gods, but they could cost you a fortune in orthodontic treatment later in life.

Don't let them get attached to a smelly rag, teddy or blanket. No amount of peace and quiet now is worth the hell of getting them off that thing when they're going to big school.

Don't tell your child that their thumb will drop off if they continue sucking; it will only spur them on to find out if it's true.

Toddler tantrum
dos and don'ts

Do use this tense moment to ask your partner whether it's OK if you buy that new dress/computer/ car that you wanted. They'll be too stressed and distracted to argue.

Do retreat to a nice quiet corner where no one can find you until the ordeal is over.

Don't be a wimp. This is a tiny child you have to stand up to, not the England Rugby Team.

Don't be defeated
– turn up the radio,
sing along and give
as good as you get.

No matter how stressed you are never say:

Anything that could be brought against you as evidence in court. You don't know how much your toddler will repeat on the witness stand.

No matter how stressed you are never say:

Rude words that they're
bound to use in front
of your partner/their
grandparents/any
number of better-behaved
children at playgroup.

A bit of birthday advice

Never forget that it's
their party and they'll
cry if they want to.

No matter how much you supervise the event, someone *will* end up in hospital. Make sure all the guests' parents have signed waivers absolving you of any legal responsibility.

Don't buy those candles
that can't be blown out.
Toddlers won't get the
joke and you'll have a
mutiny of sugar-rushing
monsters on your hands.

Avoid public embarrassment by:

Wearing an 'I'm not with that crying brat' T-shirt.

Hiring an actor to go to the same places as you and your toddler and make an even bigger scene... if that's possible.

Avoid public embarrassment by:

Buying all your groceries on the Internet. Think how much you'll save when you don't have to pay for all those things your toddler picks up and mauls.

Why it was so much better when they couldn't walk

Your family heirlooms have become grubby leaning posts for this tottering tot.

Your shoe collection is a mess of chewed, slobber-covered leather that any pup would be proud of.

You're forced to sleep on the sofa on account of you not having worked out how to open the child safety gate on the stairs.

Toddler-friendly family Christmas

Make sure dad's dressed up as Father Christmas and you leave out a glass of sherry. Feel free to top it up as much as you like.

Don't buy any toys that involve concentrated 'putting together'. You're going to be far too merry on mulled wine to make sure Part F connects to the right end of Part G.

Never volunteer your toddler to play a lead role in the local nativity play – do you really want to be held responsible for the damages caused when they pee in the manger?

Going Potty

Things your toddler will do to drive you up the wall

Go for the world record number of Twiglets that can fit up one nostril

Drop their dummy in the sandpit forcing you to wash it only to return to find them eating the sand

Repeat everything
you say until you're
forced into silence

Sure-fire ways to annoy your partner

Exclaim how hard your day was at work, when they've spent all day at home with a living, breathing tantrum.

Force them to carry an
oversized bag of 'toddler
necessities' around
all day, but forget to
bring the toddler.

Keep going on about
how you should have
got a dog instead.

The secrets to stress-free serenity

No money is too much to pay someone to look after your child – even if it is your partner.

Play grandparents off
against each other
so they're constantly
competing to be the
most loved. This way
you should only have
to spend a few weeks a
year with your toddler.

Hints from the Highchair: a Toddler's Perspective

The real reasons toddlers do what they do

Toddlers only run into the road to test the emergency stopping capabilities of drivers in your neighbourhood.

Toddlers throw their food around because they
a) have more sophisticated palates than you thought,
b) are watching their weight or
c) are working on their entry for the Turner Prize.

Toddlers put things in their mouths because they don't have handbags or spacious pockets to use as portable storage space.

Toddler talk: the truths

Toddlers actually tell you they love you to get what they want.

The first word a toddler says is the name of the person they can most easily manipulate.

The only reason toddlers
have a limited vocabulary
is so they never have
to explain themselves,
even under torture.

I'm causing a
scene because...

... according to the
Human Rights Act I have
a right to peaceful protest.

... you would too if you'd wet yourself and then were forced to carry on with the weekly shop.

I'm causing a scene because...

... it's the only way to get you to see the emotional impact this new, unfashionable haircut has caused me.

That's All
Folks!

You know your
toddler's growing
up when:

They kick up a fuss
because you won't buy
organic chocolate.

You know your toddler's growing up when:

They join an Internet
networking site.

And remember...

No tantrum can last forever. Eventually they'll tire themselves out and fall asleep. Treasure these moments – they are few and far between.

www.summersdale.com